SUICIDAL LOVE

A BOOK OF REFLECTIVE THOUGHTS AND POETRY

Books by Laneen A. Haniah

SUICIDAL LOVE: *The Kiss That Shattered My Soul*

Help, My Child Doesn't Want to Live!
How to reach your depressed, suicidal teen

Suicidal Love:
A Book of Reflective Thoughts and Poetry

How to Love a Black Man:
RESPECT HIM-2025 Edition

This Is Me!
I Don't Need Your Permission
(New memoir celebrating 50 years of life!
Pre-order now.)

Find eBooks, bundles, and specials on the author's website

www.soulah.me

Suicidal Love

A Book of Reflective Thoughts and Poetry

Laneen A. Haniah

"SouLah the Legend"

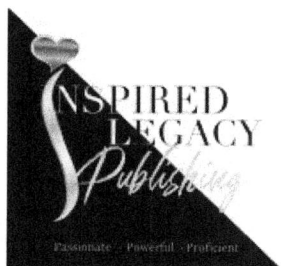

Inspired Legacy Publishing
Marietta, GA

Suicidal Love
A Book of Reflective Thoughts and Poetry

Copyright ©2022, by Laneen A. Haniah

Laneen A. Haniah
www.SouLah.me

Published September 29, 2022
Inspired Legacy Publishing, LLC
www.InspiredLegacyPublishing.com
(972) 809-8492

First Edition
ISBN: 978-1-7346633-1-0 *(paperback)*
LCCN: pending

From the series: ***Taking Your Power Back!***
1st printing 09/2022

Printed in the United States of America

Table of Contents

PREFACE

A "Side Order" of Reflections and Poems

You are about to read a potent collection of words that sum up the emotional chaos I lived in during my most intense bipolar and PTSD episodes, and all the relationship drama that came along with the instability of my mental and emotional health! I deliver my reflections in poems and wordplay related to quoted content from my associated title, *SUICIDAL LOVE: The Kiss That Shattered My Soul*. Many of the poems you will read also appear in *The Kiss That Shattered My Soul*, but in this book they are the *focus* instead of a *sidenote*.

I have listed the poems in the order they appear in the main title and have included excerpts from the chapter in which you will find them. I also share some of my thoughts about the content of the chapter and the correlating poem. You will learn insider information about my life and understand the inspiration behind each poem. I guess you could say this *Book of Reflective Thoughts and Poetry* is like being backstage in the green room with the author!

When I began writing *The Kiss That Shattered My Soul* my focus was different. The concept, motive, and content of that book slowly evolved over a two-year period as my soul took on a new identity. As I healed, I also transformed, and my reasons for drafting the book changed. My perspective changed as well, and that obviously altered how I chose to tell my story. The book became something that I never imagined—something much more beautiful.

As the project aligned with its true purpose, one of the biggest surprises for me was the growing word-count. My initial notions of writing a *quick and short* booklet is laughable now. The original draft of *The Kiss That Shattered My Soul*— which was then titled, *Take Your Power Back*—was so long that I had to divide it into parts. What started off as something meant to be an "insightful 50-page booklet", intended mainly for marketing purposes, is now pegged to be an entire series of books!

I was stressed about the intimidating size of the book at first. However, I eventually gave up on trying to temper the expanding word-count and embraced its development into what it was destined to become. I was happy with what I'd given birth to, but in the final stages of editing *The Kiss That Shattered My Soul*, I felt like something was missing. As I thumbed through the pages, it somehow felt *incomplete*. That's mind-boggling to reflect on because the book was already over 102,000 words when I had that thought. *(LOL, insanity, I know!)*

As an editor and publisher, I was satisfied. But as both a writer and an artist, I knew I could make the book more emotionally impactful. Since making a strong emotional impact was one of my main objectives for writing the book in the gripping manner I chose to narrate it, I was compelled to maximize every opportunity to create the desired impression. To turn *The Kiss That Shattered My Soul* into an overload of emotional stimuli, it needed poetry—exclusive, custom poetry that would serve as the final *exclamation mark* and *exhale* at the end of each chapter!

Adding the poetry enhanced the depth of the read to an even greater degree than I anticipated. It was like watching the climax of an action film. The hero and the antagonist were fighting to the death, and it appeared our hero was losing. But just when all hope seemed lost, she jumps up in slow-motion, with a leaping spin kick to the side of the head that knocks her opponent out cold! I know that's a bit dramatic—*but hey,* that's what it felt like to me reading the poetry at the end of the chapters! And I have been told by some people that the poetry is as impactful as the main content.

All that being said, *The Kiss That Shattered My Soul* is an intense read; it is a lot to take in. This book, **Suicidal Love: A Book of Reflective Thoughts and Poetry,** is meant to help you better appreciate and digest the content in the flagship title. It's like a *side order of reflections and poems* to make the meal that much more nourishing and enjoyable. But it's also a side order that can be served as the main course, and in this case it is being served as such.

Please let me make clear that this book is not meant to take the place of *The Kiss That Shattered My Soul,* but instead is meant to be a companion to it. I was careful not to reveal any spoilers in this little supplemental book, so it is safe to read before, during, or after the main course. In fact, I even suggest reading the two books side-by-side, allowing you to really see through my perspective as you take in each chapter. Either way, as a standalone title or as a supplement, I know you will greatly benefit from the content in this book. Enjoy!

In the power of Love,
Laneen A. Haniah
Laneen A. Haniah aka *SouLah the Legend*

PART I
The Death Of
"2017 Laneen"

Reflections...

SUICIDAL LOVE: The Kiss That Shattered My Soul is the first book in my series called, *Taking Your Power Back!* As I stated in the Preface, the book evolved into something I never imagined. It becoming a series was part of the evolution. I had previously completed the book, under the title *"Take Your Power Back"*. However, upon final editing I realized the manuscript covered too much material, and too large a timeframe to delve into what I wanted to share, so I divided it into two parts. *Part 1* was entitled as you see it here, *The Death of "2017 Laneen"*.

The Death of "2017 Laneen" is such a fitting title for *Part 1* of this series. *The Kiss That Shattered My Soul* is the story of how I allowed a relationship to strip me of my will to live. It follows my journey with a man who turned out to be an enemy to my soul. From the day we met until the day his cruelty triggered me wanting to end my life, I walk you through the pain and agony of the abuse I allowed. However, for me, my antagonist is not the focal point. The real story is how I betrayed myself.

After surviving that experience, I had to come to grips with the fact that my suicidal depression wasn't about a man. It wasn't the first time I had attempted suicide, and I knew if I didn't elevate it wouldn't be the last. To overcome the darkness within, I had to die to the version of myself that allowed him access to my heart. I had to die to the version of myself that was attracted to toxic connections and detrimental relationships. I had to die to *suicidal love*.

The Kiss That Shattered My Soul is about *The Death of 2017 Laneen*—in other words, the death of my former self.

There Once Was a Girl

There once was a girl.
The embodiment of trauma and rejection,
she unintentionally cut others
with the jagged edges of her broken soul.

She gave off an aroma,
but not that of perfume.
It was the stench of infection
from her fragmented wounds.

Both the destroyer and the destroyed,
she was the villain and the victim.
She let people in, only to be crushed.
She loved others, only to hurt them.

Because wholeness can't come from brokenness,
it was hard for her to care about others
when she didn't even care about herself.

Irreparably damaged, she could not be saved.
For the sake of all creation, she had to be put in the grave.

Irreconcilable defection—
she was deformed and ugly inside.
So, with a lethal shot of hopelessness,
she finally gave up and died.

There once was a girl, and that girl was me.
But she's dead now; may she rest in peace.

INTRODUCTION
And The Winner Is...

Excerpt from The Kiss That Shattered My Soul

...the truth is—*I WAS ALWAYS SUICIDAL, EVEN WHEN I WASN'T!* Even when I was not actively *planning* my murder, I was killing myself slowly with my daily decisions. *I saw a broken life that could not be fixed, one that was better off euthanized than spared*—and that is how I lived. Death had become the only acceptable end for me, and though I was not acting on thoughts of self-harm, my life was like *suicide on a payment plan.* I can make a comparison between premeditated murder versus manslaughter to explain this; both are crimes that cause death, just with different degrees of intent.

As I delve into the events that caused my world to cave in, I'm going to give you an overview of my *suicidal lifestyle.* I call it a *"lifestyle"* because *"suicidal thoughts and acts of self-harm are only the final stage in a long list of behaviors that will inevitably end in death."* **Suicidal depression is more than self-harm or thoughts of dying. It is living in a way that brings death to your hopes; to your purpose; and to your dreams.** The *suicidal lifestyle* is one in which you make decisions that cause you emotional harm. It is a way of living that hinders your ability to find happiness, peace, fulfillment, and even love.

Reflections…

Writing the introduction for *The Kiss That Shattered My Soul* was challenging. *How would I ease into revealing to the world that I wasn't who I appeared to be?* Very few people knew about my struggles with mental illness and suicidal depression, not even those closest to me knew how bad it really was. *How could they?* I was in denial about it myself. As I grappled with how to introduce my topic, I thought, *"Let's just rip the Band Aid off! First present yourself the way people already know you—an award-winning author and radio personality; a beautiful, dynamic, successful, loved woman who is always smiling… Yes, show them what they're used to seeing, and then snatch the veil off!"*

I felt so vulnerable writing the introduction. It would be the first time I ever shared my secret shame. Writing the introduction felt as if I took to the stage, grabbed the mic, tapped on it a couple of times, and said:

> "Excuse me everybody. I have an announcement to make. I have bipolar disorder. I have attempted suicide seven times, and the most recent was right after you saw me collect an award for being such a *'dynamic world-changer'*. This is not something that I *used* to struggle with, or something that I've *'overcome*. It is a current, daily battle. I'm sorry to disappoint you, but your *champion* is not so strong after all."

Yeah… That's what it felt like. It still kind of feels like that now. But at the very least, I can say I'm free from the pretense of allowing people to think I'm *okay* when some days I'm anything but…

I'm Not Okay

Excuse me… *I'm not okay.*
I may be smiling,
but I'm having a really bad day.

Believe it or not, I also had a bad night.
In fact, it's been a bad life,
and I'm losing my fight.

I'm losing my drive, my press, my desire to live.
I'm losing the will to keep going
if something doesn't give.

I need a hug, I need a break,
I need a breakthrough.
If I break down,
I need to know it's alright with you!

I know you prefer the version of me
that keeps it all together
and holds everyone up.
But if I'm being honest, it's a burden to me,
cuz ain't no one strong forever
and I can't pour from an empty cup!

So, I'm sorry if you can't handle it,
but this is my confession.
Most days I'm *NOT okay,*
pretending otherwise is my transgression.

Enjoying this book so far?

Please stop and take a moment to leave a 5-star review on Amazon!

Please visit https://www.amazon.com/review/create-review/edit?ie=UTF8&channel=glance-detail&asin=1734663316

Or scan the QR below

Chapter One

The Backstory

Excerpt from The Kiss That Shattered My Soul

Talking in the same calm, despondent tone, my husband spent the next three hours confessing how much he had resented me since the first month of our marriage. He explained the hateful ways he felt for me. He referenced different scenarios from our past, pointing out specific instances in which he deliberately showed his resentment toward me through his actions. He shared his opinion that "with my filthy past", I should have been grateful that any man wanted me, and that my desire to be treated with respect disgusted him. He then ended by saying that it wasn't anything that I had necessarily done wrong—he just didn't love me, *or even like me.*

I was taken aback by his words. It was not news to me that my husband wasn't in love with me. I knew the day we got married that he didn't love me, but I had no idea it ran that deep. And yet, it wasn't even him not being in love with me that bothered me the most. It was more so the implication that *he didn't even have a desire to love me!*

Reflections...

It's strange reading about how my ex-husband treated me. It's not strange because I wrote about it, or even that it happened. It's strange because just this morning he and I sat down and had breakfast together with our children, IN MY HOME. We laughed so freely as we shared some of our fun memories with the kids. He even joked about how he was too broke to hold onto me, and it was all so genuine and beautiful. As a matter of fact, he stayed with us for a few days and me and my current husband chuckled about it. The idea of my ex-husband spending the night in the same home with my new husband sounds nuts, but that really happened because we are really that free and whole!

In Chapter One of *The Kiss That Shattered My Soul*, I give you an overview of my first marriage and how it ended. Me and my ex-husband—*his name is Emmanuel, by the way*—have such a peaceful and friendly relationship now that it was heartbreaking to include our horrid past in my book. I danced around it for a while, but it just wasn't fair to my process or to my readers to leave it out. The pain I suffered in our marriage was a vast factor in my suicidal depression. Our entire relationship was founded on *suicidal love*, and it took more than 10 years for me to close all of those wounds.

Honestly, it's only as of recently that I have put all of that behind me. For so many years I saw myself through the ugliness of his perception. And even in my marriage now, I sometimes see glimpses of his old view of who I was in his eyes. There is just no way I could accurately tell my story, without explaining how being an unloved wife factored into the decisions I later made. My poem, *The Stranger in My Bed,* is such a chilling depiction of what it felt like to be married to him. There were many times I rolled over in bed and looked at him, wondering where my *real husband* had been taken.

That being said, I want to assure you that we are good now. Emmanuel is a beautiful soul. He has repented. He has changed and his kindness toward me and our children has been a great part of my healing process. He wasn't the best husband, but he's a good dad, and he's a good friend.

The Stranger in My Bed

I awaken in a cold sweat,
staring in terror at the dark figure that lingers near the edge of my bed.
He stands over me,
his piercing black eyes sending a shooting pain to my head.
My heart pounds,
as, through shallowed breaths I whisper,
"Who are you?"

He doesn't answer.
Instead, he grabs my hand and places it on his chest.
But there's a hollow echo where his heart should rest.
I gasp and snatch my hand away as I scream!

He leans in closer, with a menacing smile.
*"Of course you know me. I've been here for a while.
We walked down the aisle. We said I do.
You belong to me, and I belong to you."*

I, at last, recognize his face and discern his voice.
He looks like the man I married, but I know this wasn't my choice.
I've been tricked, I've been duped; it's the old bait and switch!
This can't be, this ain't him; there must be a glitch!

Suddenly I wake up; it was only a dream!
My husband lay next to me, deep in his sleep.
I frantically shake him to wake him, saying,
"Babe, I had a terrible nightmare, and you were there!"

He opens his piercing black eyes,
sending a shooting pain to my head.
My husband is him;
he is the stranger in my bed.

Chapter Two

Got Me Feeling Some Way

Excerpt from The Kiss That Shattered My Soul

...There was indeed a "divine connection", yet not a profitable one. Not every "spiritual connection" comes into your life to elevate you. Spiritual energy can be *good or evil.* It can come from *a Source of Light* or *a source of darkness*, and either source can orchestrate *divine appointments.*

Please be aware that both demons and angels come to us from the spirit world, and both foster strong "vibes" and "connections"! My "divine connection" with Keb was *from the dark side*; it was spiritual brokenness meets spiritual lust. Keb was operating under the power of a predator spirit, and I was operating under the spirit of prey. But the connection didn't necessarily feel that way to me at the time. I was at such a low point in my life that I was **desperate for connection**, no matter what was attached to it.

Reflections...

I think one of the greatest shortcomings of humanity is our lack of understanding of the spirit world. Many people either ignore the spirituality of our existence or misunderstand and misappropriate its power! Being "spiritual" is so "trendy" now-a-days. But we don't know what the hell—*I mean that literally*—we're getting into most of the times!

In Chapter Two of *The Kiss That Shattered My Soul*, I introduce you to my antagonist, who I call "KEB". Keb and I "connected" instantly. I mean, it was *lust at first sight!* It was for him anyway. *For me...* I really didn't know what it was. I just knew from the moment he laid eyes on me; he completely bombarded my soul. He immediately trespassed on my heart, but out of my brokenness, I misinterpreted that as a *divine connection* and much-needed validation.

I was usually such a closed-off person. It was hard for a man to get anywhere with me, yet alone near the sacredness of my core. The way Keb stormed in and took over was something I had never experienced. Unfortunately, I confused that *for leadership, for care, for love...* I called it everything except what it was—a demonic force—a dark energy that came to desecrate and destroy the light in me.

There is a scripture in the Bible that says, *"The thief comes only in order to steal, kill, and destroy. (John 10:10, LEB)"* Keb was an enemy of my very existence. He was sent to do what those types of enemies are assigned to do—*steal my virtue, kill my light, and destroy my soul.*

I don't use "Keb's" real name in the book, but that was not done for his sake. His real name is Kevin, and I have no problem sharing that because there is no desire on my part to protect his identity. The only reason I used a fake identity is because I couldn't stomach seeing his name over and over again as I wrote and edited my manuscript. He does not deserve to live out in the open space of my mind, and his name does not deserve a place in my legacy!

Just FYI, K.E.B. stands for **K**evin's **E**xtreme **B**ullsh*t... *And believe me, that's all he turned out to be.* It feels so good to be able to clearly see that now and be free of the spell he cast over me!!!

Divine Connection

Excuse me sir, I'm in need of a friend.
You look kind of scary, every now and again,
but the vibe is so strong, I'll still let you in.

You see, I'm desperate for connection.
So, I will take that chance.
We gonna have this dance.
I don't want romance.
But if that's what it costs me,
I might risk that too.

Navigating through
the dark corridors of your soul,
I search for light.
If I find none,
I'm no worse off than I was last night.
Or the night that has lasted far too long.
For the hope you'll do me right,
I'll endure your wrong.

Never mind the detection of infection
in the projection of your affection!
This is a divine connection
that absolutely demands my protection!

But wait—
I need your name if we gonna go to that next level.
What was that?
Last name, "in-disguise", first name, "devil".

Chapter Three

The "Open Relationship"

Excerpt from The Kiss That Shattered My Soul

Me and Keb's girl had a trauma bond that I honored. I had been that "side-chick" *crumpled up on the floor, sobbing loudly and barely able to breathe.* I knew what it was like for my married man to suddenly get *zapped by the integrity wand.* Men often get a visit from the "integrity fairy" when side p*ssy begins to cost them more than they want to pay for it! It's then that they clarify you were just a dispensable convenience along their path. I had been there more than once.

Everyone can sympathize with the wronged wife, but **only someone who has been there can understand the darkness of being a dismissed mistress.** *I KNOW WHAT THAT FEELS I IKE.* I can feel It even now as I write this...

Reflections...

I talk very openly in *The Kiss That Shattered My Soul* about my long-term relationship with a married man. There was a time that I was known as an *icon of sexual purity*. After all, I am the woman who wrote *The Spirits of Sexual Perversion Reference Book*, and *STDs: Sexually Transmitted Demons*. I am the woman who was known all over the internet as *Dr. Intimacy*. I am the person you called when you were battling lust demons, sexual addictions, and relationship issues. I was THAT woman! Knowing that made it grueling for me to share about my affair.

As difficult as it was to open up about it, it was even more difficult to live through! Transparency is not hard for me. I think I have mastered transparency. It's knowing that I did the things that I must now be "transparent" about that I struggle with. Having said that, I realize that my ease with transparency is uncommon. I understand that most people don't ever want their shameful secrets known. *Shoot,* they don't even want to face them.

I'm sensitive to this, but it does create a conflict when I'm telling my testimonies. Sometimes for me to tell my truth means exposing somebody else's lie. I faced such a dilemma when drafting *The Kiss That Shattered My Soul.* In Chapter Three, I delve into the backstory of Keb's relationships; meaning I expose not only him, but who he was in relationship with as well. That wasn't an easy thing to do, and I re-wrote that chapter so many times.

I kept stripping away details until I was down to the bare bones of the story. Had I said any less, I might as well have left it out. But just as in the case of my horrid past with my ex-husband, it wasn't fair to my process or to my readers to omit the details I share in Chapter Three. My history with married men played a great role in my suicidal love cycles, and the story I share in Chapter Three is very relevant.

I don't want to give away any spoilers, so you'll have to read *The Kiss That Shattered My Soul* to understand what I mean by this. But I want broken women—the so-called side chicks of the world—to know that I understand their pain. *Whenever you're ready **My Soul Sister**, let's talk about how to raise your worth and get out of the situation you've trapped yourself in. I know it's hard, but there's something better for you out there, I promise you there is.*

My Soul Sister

You are my sister.
Not by birth, by blood, or even adoption.
But by experience, by understanding,
and through life's happenings as a painful concoction.

It's a trauma bond that we share.
A bond of abandonment and rejection,
not measuring up and being the second selection.

We are broken women, wounded souls,
and misunderstood passion.
We love hard but wrong,
like a sad love song,
and get judged for our reactions.

Not *"actions"* but *"reactions"*.
Because we didn't seek these married men.
We didn't want this life of sin.

We were predisposed by our *non-fathers*
to settle for less and never expect the best,
because that kind of love is reserved for *the rest*.

The worthy women of the world, which we are not.
Discarded like an old tissue full of snot,
we take whatever we can get because that's our lot.

We are soul sisters.
Not by birth or by blood,
but through a trauma bond of rejection.
So, I receive you with love…

From the book *Suicidal Love* © 2022, Laneen A. Haniah. All rights reserved.

Chapter Four

The Night Of The Shift

Excerpt from The Kiss That Shattered My Soul

For the first time, I let my guards down and relented in Keb's presence. My normal resistance was depleted. I was vulnerable as I rested in **the hope of his hug**, attempting to absorb its non-existent healing power. *But… Keb was Keb*, and it was only a short-lived moment of tranquility. My soul was snatched back into the harshness of my reality when he slid his hands into the opening between my skin and the loose-fitting waistband on my jeans!

I don't know if anyone ever tried to teach Keb to treat women like his sister or his mother because he always handled me like a sex object, even though I had always carried myself modestly in his presence. I'd done nothing to give Keb the impression it was okay to touch me in that way. Instead, I had clarified to him repeatedly that I did not have the desire or the willingness to have sex with him. Yet, what should have been a *healing embrace* turned out to be an *ensnaring embrace!*

The audacity of his disrespectful behavior should have taken precedence, but **I needed a hug at all costs—so I let it happen.**

Despite Keb's brazen behavior, he had secured both,
his place in my heart and his place in my bed.
*With a TOXIC HUG—our **Suicidal Love** affair had begun.*

Reflections...

Chapter Four of *The Kiss That Shattered My Soul* is so raw! I tell the story of the turning point in my relationship with Keb and narrate it as if it were part of a novel. It reads like a movie. There was no other way to write it and really do it justice. It was just that EPIC and it feels surreal to me when I revisit it.

If I could take back a day in my life, I think I'd take that day back. I don't really believe in having regrets, so I can't honestly say I'd change anything that happened. But I can say that had *the night of the shift* never happened, I never would have ended up where I did with Keb. We continued to *play the game*, but trust me, he could have already yelled "check mate!" that night. It was a done deal from that precise moment in time...

I won't give away the story, but dang!

I have no more to say about that night or Chapter Four. The poem *Toxic Affection* sums it up nicely because *suicidal love* is drawn to toxic affection. When you're used to poison, poison is good to your tastes. Although it's killing you, you become numb to the pain and even see it as gain.

Toxic Affection

Your toxic affection feels so good.
Poison me baby; poison me with your *"would"*.

"I 'would' love you if only I cared.
I 'would' care if only I could.
I 'could' care if only I wanted to…
…But—I don't!
You're just a piece of meat
that I want to beat with my meat."

You say it to me plainly,
as you show me your intentions.
But it all sounds so sweet
to my bloodshot ears,
soothing my fears,
with your toxic inventions—
of lust that's made to look like love,
of abuse that's made to feel like comfort.

But your conventions are so convincing
that I'm not even wincing,
cuz I keep rinsing
your words and actions
to make them feel justified.
This love is like suicide!

I'm in love with your toxic affection.
It feels so good that I'm in total subjection...

Chapter Five

Escaping The Abyss

Excerpt from The Kiss That Shattered My Soul

When you feel like you're dying, you're dying to feel anything else! You will accept any kind of abuse or mistreatment that presents itself to you, as long as it gives you hope. Keb offered me relief from longing for death and gave me the hope that I ached for; and therefore, I felt indebted to him **...because he had carelessly placed himself between me and death.** That's not what either of us signed up for, but it's what our relationship became.

The reality of my circumstances was grim. I had to choose between two evils. Even though Keb was a predator, he was a much safer option than *the abyss*. I guess when it came down to it...

It was suicidal sadness versus suicidal love.

Reflections...

Chapter Five might be my favorite chapter in *The Kiss That Shattered My Soul*. I disclose a theory—a revelation if you will—that I truly believe came from God Himself! I call it *The Laws of Emotional Energy.* I use the theory to really teach you about your emotional health. I explain how mood disorders, such as bipolar, affect our emotional balance. I explain how we gain *emotional momentum,* and how we get shifted out of it.

Up until Chapter Five in the book, I feel so lost. My behavior didn't make any sense. Why I would allow someone to treat me the way that I allowed Keb to treat me was unfathomable, and it made me angry at myself until I wrote and understood Chapter Five. I explain with precision and clarity exactly what happened on my emotional plane on *the night of the shift*—and suddenly the whole story makes sense. I can almost guarantee you that your own life and crazy behavior will make more sense to you if you take the time to really understand and retain the information in Chapter Five!

Without understanding, you may continue to feel like you're living under the cruel regime of *The Abyss.* When I wrote that poem it flowed from my pen like oil. I'm so familiar with the terror of suicidal depression that it took only minutes to express it in a poem. When I showed the poem to my children, my son Ben said:

> *"That's so deep and dark. I can't imagine going through reality living like that every day. That's like living in a black whole, trying to escape but you can't see because it's pitch black, and the power of gravity is so immense that it's tearing you apart and sucking you in deeper and deeper until you get to the center... The point where all hope is lost, and all will is gone and you're just ready to die!"*

No baby, you *can* imagine. If you can describe it that accurately, you must have at least got close enough to *press your nose up against the glass to see it...*

The Abyss

Spiraling down in a black void of depression,
I feel your power.

Your grip around my throat
muffles my screams and labors my breathing.
The sound of my own heart beating
deafens my ears to the voices around me.
No one can discern my cries for help,
nor can I discern their reasoning.
My vision is blurred
from an uninterrupted flow of tears.
My head pounds from the same.
Raging thoughts abuse my mind,
as I try to sleep.
And even in my dreams,
You Find Me.

My body is numb to all sensation,
and though I long to be touched,
I can never feel it.
There is no comfort,
there is no peace,
there is no hope.
For you have taken over my life
and consumed me.

***There is no escape from
THE ABYSS.***

Chapter Six

A Lifetime Of Trauma

Excerpt from The Kiss That Shattered My Soul

There are things that happen to us in life that we have no control over, things that devastate us to our core and forever transform us.

Whereas we may physically survive our traumas, often, something dies on the inside. There couldn't be a more poignant example of this than the sexual assault I suffered as a child. It damaged me in a way that showed up in my behavior deep into my adulthood. It factored into why I married a man who didn't love me. It factored into why I was willing to be a long-term mistress. It factored into why I allowed Keb to have access to me. What I want you to see is that sometimes your "bad behavior" is really an infected heart-wound, leaking pus—*it is often the "dead tissue" in your soul.*

This is the reason we sometimes have suppressed memories. Pain that deep is hard to *live with*; and so, it is common for the brain to block out a memory so traumatizing that to walk with the knowledge of it would be unbearable. It is like how people pass out in response to an overload of physical pain. Extreme physical pain often causes people to just "fall asleep". The brain's solution for insufferable pain is to simply put that pain to sleep. This can be the case whether the pain is physical or emotional.

Reflections...

There are two chapters in *The Kiss That Shattered My Soul* that almost killed me to write, and this is one of them. In fact, it was THE HARDEST CHAPTER FOR ME TO WRITE. I cried incessantly as I wrote and edited Chapter Six. I recall a day that I nearly passed out from crying so hard. *(I'm tearing up now as I remember that moment.)*

It was at this point that I almost regretted writing the book. It was at this point that I wanted to delete it from my computer and go write a happy children's book or work on my next album or paint a landscape or renovate my house or learn how to fly a plane... ***absolutely anything*** *except finish writing that book!!!*

I remember screaming at God that day as I cried so hard. I don't normally feel any type of anger toward God, but in that moment I was a little peeved with Him. I'm embarrassed to admit that, but it happens in every relationship on occasion, and that day was my *occasion* to be mad at *My Friend.* In Chapter Six, I sum up some of the most painful and traumatic events of my life. I think seeing them all laid out, crammed into one chapter full of blackness and blood was overwhelming, and that is what caused what I was feeling toward The One who had created me.

It is not uncommon for people to marvel at my life story. There have been times that people actually thought I was making stuff up because it was so unimaginable to them that one person could experience so many different traumas in one lifetime. But I honestly never really felt the shock and awe that others experience when they hear my story until I wrote Chapter Six. I don't know why it took me cramming it all into a chapter in a book for it to finally hit me how tragic my life has been, but now that I've seen it, *I can't unsee it!* Believe me, I wish it was a made-up life. But unfortunately, my story needs no embellishment. It is more gripping than any Hollywood script!

But I'm glad that I can finally feel all the pain that my brain had "put to sleep". Pain means I'm still alive, and it means that my soul is fighting to heal itself. I was in an *emotional coma*, but now I'm fully awake and God is showing me every day that there is purpose in my pain. It is *Beautiful, Purposeful Pain.* By the way, this is by far my favorite poem in the book. Imagine that. The most painful chapter, produced the most beautiful conclusion...

Beautiful, Purposeful Pain

I almost gave up,
because I couldn't stop hurting.
I kept trying to grow,
but instead, I was reverting.

Plunging into darkness,
like a never-ending free fall.
But then I heard His voice,
because no matter what, He sees all.

He pulled me from the bottom,
I landed softly in His love.
He then whispered in my ear,
"My daughter, please don't give up."

"I make all things beautiful,
in the proper time.
I make all pain worth it,
like crushing grapes for wine.

Like trees die in winter,
to blossom in the Spring.
And a naked baby bird,
will soon spread its feathered wings.

Like an embryo that's formless,
becomes an infant child.
And a berry that can't be eaten,
nourishes the wild.

So are you my daughter,
not yet revealed.
But your day of favor comes,
in a time that pain will yield.

I will pull back the curtain on failure,
and you'll see that from the beginning,
when it seemed that you were losing,
in truth, you were always winning!

At times when it was darkest,
My Sword was at its sharpest.
And when you were at your worse,
My Spirit was breaking a curse!

So, my child, please don't quit,
you have it within, to take these hits!
I'm making you strong, and though it's scary,
the hurt won't compare, to the gift you'll carry!

And while I cannot promise you a pain free life,
I can promise you purpose.
I can also promise you, I'll be by your side,
and my angels will be at your service.

I won't waste a single tear from your story,
as I execute my plan,
to bring you honor and get My Glory,
and the ending will be grand!

It only requires that you never give up,
just hold on to My hand.
And when you feel too weak,
you can rest in my strength.
I'll carry you until you can stand."

Chapter Seven

Emotional Prostitution

Excerpt from The Kiss That Shattered My Soul

...My body count is way above average, and it left me feeling like filthy, damaged goods. I didn't think any man would ever want me, so when my first husband offered to marry me, I literally jumped at the chance! I had put my promiscuous life behind me before my husband and I met, but when we started dating, it had only been three months since I'd last had sex. He, on the other hand, had six years of abstinence under his belt. I can't even explain to you how dirty I felt in his presence. I thought to myself, *"Why would a 'clean man' like him want a 'dirty whore' like me?"* So, even knowing that he didn't love me on our wedding day; having him was more than I felt I deserved. *Loved or not, it was redemption to me.*

The voice of my hidden self was drowning out the voice of my free will. My hidden self constantly spoke to the dead places in my soul. Like a ringing in the ears that never goes away, it kept reminding me I was the same dirty *pass-around-girl* that I had always been. And everybody knows—*whores don't get to have a voice; they must show up and put out for whoever demands it.* Somewhere inside of myself, I was still living in that false-reality.

Reflections…

Some chapters are hard to write because they're painful, and some are just hard to face because they're shameful. Chapter Seven was *hard to face;* it was hard to face for so many reasons. First off, coming to grips with how little self-worth I had was almost sickening. I truly imagined that I deserved the mistreatment I received from people because of skewed religious beliefs, personal failures, predators, and persecution. And second, because of how I fell away from truths that I knew, truths that would have kept me safe from some of the pain I suffered.

You will never be happy living a life that falls short of what you believe to be right. You cannot violate your morals and principals then scream *injustice* when others violate you! Please, don't miss what I'm saying. No one has the right to violate you, but if YOU VIOLATE YOURSELF, you open the door for others to do the same. Seeing how I opened the door for my predators to come in and eat at my table is painful to relive. But it's even more painful when I understand the reason behind my actions.

Yes, I invited them in, but it's only because I didn't see myself as deserving of anything better. Even as I try to hold myself accountable for my poor choices, It's hard to charge it to my account! Maybe it's more like, I find myself "guilty as charged", but due to extenuating circumstances, I grant myself "time-served" and on-going probation. Yes, I did the crime, but I was never in my right mind. When a person can write a poem like *The Clearance Bin*, and mean every word of it, there is no way that person is in their right mind. In fact, I don't even think I was *fit to stand trial!*

This poem is a favorite when I do shows and interviews. It hits every time. Sadly, I think it's because so many people can relate.

The "Clearance Bin"

What is my worth? *Have I any value at all?*
How could I expect anyone to pay for a scrap so small?

Like a damaged item in a retail store,
I've been tossed into the *"clearance bin"*.
I've been picked over and left behind,
like an old and imperfect *has-been*.

I am bruised fruit. I am left out meat.
I am expired milk. I am dirty sheets.
I am returned shoes, worn and run down.
I am a used white shirt, torn and dingy brown.
I am a broken toy, a game with missing pieces.
I am an "open box" item full of roach feces.
I am a cracked-screen TV; a laptop that won't charge.
I am a beautiful, intelligent woman,
with a past that's way too large.

Too grand, too overwhelming, too nasty,
too unforgivable, too vastly—
disgusting and shameful, mistrusting, and painful.

In fact, I *owe you* for your mere consideration.
I'll even pay you to take me if you'll be my salvation.
Because clearance bin items eventually end up in the trash.
If no one finds them valuable, they are incinerated to ash.

Save me from extinction, save me from obscurity.
You don't even have to love me, just tolerate my impurity...

Chapter Eight

Black Girl, Be My Friend

Excerpt from The Kiss That Shattered My Soul

Something in me believed that having a female "bestie" would alleviate all my *Black girl issues*. I harbored the insecurity that *all Black women secretly hated me; the fear that one of them might suddenly try to kill me for no reason; the feeling that not even one of them would ever consider me worthy of being called "best friend"*. **To make it all stop hurting, I just needed one Black sister-friend— *a BEST FRIEND.***

My past traumas had created a deep-seated need to be "accepted" by Black women. I had experienced just as much rejection and heartbreak from Black girls and women as I had from Black men. I was bullied growing up; *teased, hated, and beat on for no reason*. I was the "reject in the group" — *the girl invited to the party by "the mean girls" just so they could laugh at me*. I was accused of having sex with boys I had never touched; made fun of for my freakish appearance; and every time I thought I had a loyal friend she would turn on me. *(Like the next-door neighbor who tried to kill me.)*

I longed and ached for that emptiness in my life to be filled. I wanted some *Black Queen* to post me up on her Instagram and Facebook pages with the caption, *"this is my bestie"*. Or maybe even, *"this is my ride or die b*tch!"* Yes! I would have even loved to be called *"the 'B' word"* in that capacity! I wanted a Black sister-friend more than anything. I wanted it more than money, fame, or fortune. I wanted it more than a husband or a house. I wanted it more than anything—*to be loved by a Black woman as her BEST FRIEND.*

Reflections...

My feelings about Chapter Eight border on "embarrassing". I fought myself on including this chapter and what it reveals about my inner brokenness. *Did I really have to dive this deep into my infected soul and show the world my leaking wounds?* This wound stinks, it is infected to the point of necrosis! No! I did not want to unpack this in front of an audience. *But...*

...Once again, my longing for transparency and being true to my process and my reader won out. My "Black girl issues" are just as bad as, if not worse than, my "Daddy issues". *How could I leave this chapter out and still be fair to my reader?* And then I also thought, *"If I'm dealing with this, I know others must be going through it too!"* Maybe my courage will open a much-needed dialogue that will help women heal their relationships with each other. *I don't know...* But it's out there now and I can't take it back, *so... Whatever...*

No matter how it goes, my *Black girl issues* are a significant part of my *Suicidal Love* saga, and they will play an even bigger role in *Part 2* of this saga. If you ladies out there reading this can relate to my longing for a female bestie, please don't leave me hanging! I don't think this chapter is going to stop feeling embarrassing until I know I didn't *publicly drain this wound* for no reason. Please, *Black Girl, Black Girl, Be My Friend!* Let's be besties!

Black Girl, Black Girl, Be My Friend!
(in the voice of my inner child)

Black girl, Black girl, be my friend!
I'm smart, I'm kinda pretty, and I have lots of toys.
Let's make a private clubhouse and not invite the boys!

Black girl, Black girl, be my friend!
We can have a sleepover and do each other's hair.
I'll make you lots of goodies and show you that I care!

Black girl, Black girl, be my friend!
We can dress alike, talk alike, and walk alike too.
I'll give up who I am to be just like you!

Black girl, Black girl, be my friend!
I'll give you my money, I'll give you my time.
You can have everything as long as you're mine!

Black girl, Black girl, be my friend!
You don't need nobody else, cuz I'll never make you blue.
I'll write you letters and poems, and I'll even sing to you!

Black girl, Black girl, be my friend!
I'll always have your back and I'll be by your side.
And if anyone attacks you, I'll make 'em wish they died!

Black girl, Black girl, be my friend!
I'll be loyal and true for our whole lives long,
just be my BEST FRIEND, so I won't be alone!
I won't ask much; I just want to be accepted—
cuz I've lost my self-esteem, and I don't know where I left it...

Chapter Nine

Let's Get Married!

Excerpt from The Kiss That Shattered My Soul

Due to my "daddy deficit"; the rejection of being an illegitimate child; and my deep-seated passion to be a wife; by the time I started having sex at 15—*I wanted to marry every guy I became infatuated with.* If I felt like a guy had even *slight potential* to be a husband, I went "all-in" on the relationship from the first flirty glance. I was so eager to become that *perfect wife* I had always dreamed of being that I didn't bother to vet a relationship before I gave every piece of my heart and soul to it.

As I'm sure you can imagine, this led to repeated heartbreak and the ebbing away of my hope that my childhood dream would ever come true. Furthermore, I was often in situations in which I was fighting to be "picked", because I was in so many relationships with committed or married men. *And we all know how that goes...* I found myself on the losing side of that battle 98% of the time. This eventually led me to believe that I simply *was not good enough.*

When I finally got married, I was sent a man who was **incapable of loving me**... On the day he put me out of my home, I felt like all of creation was laughing and jeering at me. *I was nothing. I was nobody. Even when I was finally "picked", I still was not "chosen".* You cannot imagine the extensive damage this did to my hidden self. It all factored into *what I allowed* in my relationships. It had been "proven" that I had no worth or value as a wife. *Life had taught me that **I better take whatever I could get and be satisfied...***

Reflections…

In Chapter Nine, I tell the story of how badly I wanted to get married from the age of three. I remember it so vividly, my longing to be a doting wife to an adoring husband. I often wonder if all little girls want to get married as bad as I did growing up. I mean, I know it's a common thing for little girls to desire marriage, but are they absolutely consumed and obsessed with it like I was? *Is that even normal?*

It doesn't seem right because my obscene longing for marriage harmed me by warping my view of dating and relationships. I could never go on normal dates with guys. It was hard to even have platonic male friends because every *penis on the planet* that I made any kind of connection with was a potential husband. All males from the ages of 14 to 50 were potential husbands to me!

It's crazy to go through life as a single woman thinking that every man could be your husband. It occupied 98% of my brain space and prevented me from enjoying singleness. I could not be alone. At any given time I had a man in my life and in my bed. And the funny thing is, the more relationships I got into, the further away I was from the marriage I longed for, until I didn't even want marriage anymore! It's a miracle I'm married today. That was all a God thing. I had given up on it, *but He didn't give up on me.*

Whenever people read the poem, *Here Comes the Bride*, the response is always the same — *"Dang!"* That poem is so dark and poignant, but I promise you it's 100% accurate. Now women ask me how I "landed" my husband. *(I hate that terminology, but I'm using their language.)* They want to know how I overcame such darkness to enjoy a healthy marriage. I could say a lot about that; I could write a book about that… *Oh wait…* I did write a book about that!

If you want to know how I got where I am today please read, ***How to Love a Black Man: RESPECT HIM.*** You can find it on Amazon or my website www.SouLahtheLegend.com. And for all my friends reading this who aren't Black… *First,* I promise that you will get really helpful relationship insight from reading that book, no matter your race, because the principles are universal. *Second,* I am working, as we speak, on a version that is not race-specific. Please join my mailing list to find out when it becomes available. I don't want anyone to be left out. I got you! But for now, get How to Love a Black Man if you want to be marriage-ready!

Here Comes the Bride...

Here comes the bride, all dressed in white,
an innocent little girl, full of joy and light.

Here comes the bride, all dressed in hope,
she dreams of love and marriage in the fullness of its scope.

Here comes the bride, all dressed in zeal,
determined to keep dreaming until her fantasy is real.

Here comes the bride, all dressed in worry,
it's taking longer than expected and her vision's getting blurry.

Here comes the bride, all dressed in frustration,
because when she finally says, *"I do"* it is a loveless mutation.

Here comes the bride, all dressed in tears,
painful years of loneliness have reinforced her fears.

Here comes the bride, all dressed in despair,
In the anguish of rejection, she turns to an affair.

Here comes the bride, all dressed in blood,
the wounds of her abusers have made her feel unloved.

Here comes the bride, all dressed in black,
she's given everything, but no one has given back.
Her childish dream is dead, and she believes in love no more.
Tragedy and trauma have crushed her to the core!

Enjoying this book?

Please stop and take a moment to leave a 5-star review on Amazon!

Please visit https://www.amazon.com/review/create-review/edit?ie=UTF8&channel=glance-detail&asin=1734663316

Or scan the QR below

Chapter Ten

#MeToo

Excerpt from The Kiss That Shattered My Soul

...These concerns continued to *flash a proverbial stop sign* whenever I tried to convince myself that I should give in to having intercourse with Keb. Since I was so torn, I kept warning Keb of the dangers of continuing to *drag us toward the bedroom*. No matter how far we had taken things, I always offered him a gracious way out. I made it clear that it was still okay for us to go back to just being friends and business partners. I wanted Keb to be completely *sober-minded* about crossing that line with me because I knew once he penetrated me, it would **irreversibly alter everything.**

Unfortunately, even with all my great insight, I was torn between what I felt was best for everyone else and what I "perceived" I needed for myself. No matter how much I pled, Keb made it implicitly clear that if I did not have sex with him, I was going to lose him altogether. **It was all or nothing for him**. Keb was too fixated on having sex with me to let it go at that point, and I was too fixated on him to let him go. As much as I wanted him to make a different choice, *I felt like I was at his mercy.*

Reflections...

There are the chapters in *The Kiss That Shattered My Soul* that were the hardest for me to write, and then there are those that are the hardest on my readers. Chapter Ten is very triggering for many of my readers. It is graphic, vulgar, and violent... It's gut-wrenching really. It was definitely one of the more challenging chapters for me. It was a pretty simple story to write, but it was challenging to read it afterward.

You must understand that I do all of my own writing and most of my editing. On average, a manuscript has to be revised seven times before it is ready for publishing. And for every revision, you may have to read the text up to ten times to get it right. Imagine reliving some of the worst moments of your life, over and over again, in slow, painstaking, graphic detail. When people complain about reading Chapter Ten, I think to myself, *"Just be glad you didn't have to write it!"*

To be honest, after reading Chapter Ten so many times, I refused to write a poem for it at first. Chapter Ten sickened me—I mean it literally made me nauseous to the point that I couldn't eat while I worked on it. To write a custom poem for each chapter meant that I had to revisit the text and I just wouldn't do it. I have an earlier copy of *The Kiss That Shattered My Soul* sitting right here next to me with no poem for Chapter Ten!

But I somehow found the courage to get it written, and it turned out to be what I would consider the "flagship poem" for the entire book. If all of these poems were on an album, the poem *SUICIDAL LOVE* would be the featured single. This poem underscores the volume of the manuscript. It succinctly summarizes everything I want to teach you about suicidal love. And when you read it at the conclusion of Chapter Ten, it hits home so hard.

I truly applaud myself for rising to the occasion to finish my process. I left no page unturned. I left no assignment undone.

SUICIDAL LOVE

I love how you abuse and mishandle me.
I love how you confuse and dismantle me.
Cuz I can't think straight when I'm around you.
And I call it infatuation,
when in fact it's manipulation.
It's a dark magic called **lust,**
a wicked spell that defrauds me into trust.
It gets me to drop my guard and breaks my walls down,
so you can take over with aggressive passion,
that feels as if it's both love and harassment.
Your guise is fantastic!

You're a master at what you do.
But I wouldn't brag if I were you,
because I was an easy target.

I saw you with your gun
and didn't even try to run.
When you showed me your forked tongue,
I still let you kiss me.
When you denigrated my worth,
I allowed you to diss me.
I put up my hands in surrender,
offered you my heart so sweet and tender.
I let you embrace me today,
knowing you'd reject me tomorrow.
I flashed a false smile with a soul full of sorrow.
Because your words molest my heart,
and your touches bring me shame.
Yet, I risk everything I am,
with little hope of any gain.

You tell me that you love me,
but your actions say you don't.
Instead, they prove you hate me,
but let you go, I won't.
That's Suicidal Love.

It's Suicidal Love
because I love you more than I love myself.
I love you to my own detriment,
even at the expense of my mental health.
And since I really don't love me at all,
I celebrate you and your disrespectful gall.

I love all your lies and deception.
I love all of your fake validation
and your slippery salutations.
You know just what to say to make me weak,
so you can sweep me off my feet,
and disempower me until defeat.

And, although you destroy me,
I stay.
Although your pleasure is pain,
I show up anyway.
Though this relationship is killing
all my hopes and all my dreams;
to die is what I'm after,
so you didn't really need no schemes.

Cuz if I'm being honest…
I'm *willing* to love you TO DEATH.

Because That's What Suicidal Love does.

Chapter Eleven

The Aftermath

Excerpt from The Kiss That Shattered My Soul

Refusing to stop and address the source of my depression, I had driven myself deeply into a dangerous, acute manic episode. I knew at some point it would be followed by a severe depressive episode. Even with me giving so little regard to my bipolar diagnosis back then, I had a keen awareness of my high/low cycles. The higher I went, and the longer I stayed in the high of the mania—the lower I fell and the harder I crashed when it was over!

In case I did not explain it well, **emotional momentum shifts are sudden and severe.** It takes FORCE to shift energy. When that force is encountered, the shift is *instantaneous and drastic!* Think of it like a ball being thrown against a wall. If the ball hits the wall hard enough, the force of the impact sends the ball flying in another direction, with speed and power. The ball doesn't *slowly* turn and *gently* come back to you; IT FLIES BACK AT YOU WITH SUDDEN AND DANGEROUS FORCE!

This is what an *emotional momentum shift* looks like, and I could see the wall I was about to hit. **I knew I was going to hit HARD whenever I came down off my *Keb high*; and I was terrified of what that would look like and how it would play out!** As I previously mentioned: After *the night of the shift,* my conscious awareness, TOTALLY, COMPLETELY, and UTTERLY revolved around **escaping the abyss**. I lived each day to avoid plummeting into the darkness. At any cost to myself, to my destiny, and to those around me—*I was always running for my life.*

Reflections...

As you move through the chapters in *The Kiss That Shattered My Soul*, you inch closer to the day that I was ready to commit suicide. To me, it is like watching someone bump and roll down the side of a steep mountain, knowing they are unlikely to survive when they hit the bottom, and yet being helpless to do anything for them. By the time you get to Chapter Eleven, you really start to get a clear view of just how emotionally sick I was—*or at least I hope you do.*

I tried to portray it clearly in my writing how desperately close I was to death because I could feel it every waking moment. I was gasping for air at that point in my story. I had been "running" for a long time, and I knew I couldn't go much longer. I don't know what I supposed was going to happen. I guess I was hoping for some type of miracle. I just wanted to wake up one morning and be living the life of my dreams, but I knew that was only a fantasy.

I had no choice but to keep running, as fast and as hard as I could. Running was the only thing that could "save me". But really, I was just delaying the inevitable. The poem, *Running for My Life!* speaks to that reality I lived in, especially when you read it at the end of the chapter. When you read it within the context of the rest of the book, you realize that it was more than me just running *away from the abyss*. It was also me running into Keb, thinking he was going to be my salvation. I wasn't just running *from* something; I was also running *to* something. But as it turns out, they were one in the same; they both led to the same inevitable end.

Running for My Life!

I keep pretending I'm okay,
and it's the only thing I'll say.
I'll show you my bandages,
so you won't see what they're covering.
Because I know what my damage is
and can't ever see me recovering.

Black tumors all throughout my soul,
like inoperable cancer.
"How long do I have left?"
Was the question to the answer,
"I'm sorry, but it could be any day now.
We're all out of options and know-how."

So, I live swift, free, and LOUD.
If I move fast enough, maybe I can outpace this cloud!
Escaping the abyss, running for my life;
trying to resist, the urge to grab that freaking knife!
To cut into my wrist deep and slow, watch the blood flow,
watch the pain drain, relieve my brain strain.

But...
...I don't do it,
cuz your fabrications give me hope
and get me through it.

So, I'm gonna hold on to them as long as I can;
let them sustain me for an indefinite span.
Because any lifeline will do when you're dying.
So, it's either hold onto you—
or admit that I'm lying...

Chapter Twelve

The Hotel Humiliation

Excerpt from The Kiss That Shattered My Soul

Being molested by my lesbian babysitter did some deep damage to my psyche. Whatever changes took place in my brain during that time produced unnatural sexual urges and responses in me. This meant that I did not always respond to sexual stimulation the same way; mainly because I couldn't always tell where my sexual arousal was originating.

When I truly wanted to be with a man, I felt a genuine sense of arousal. But there were other times my sexual arousal felt dirty and perverted. Sometimes I would have urges that almost seemed to *come out of nowhere* because there was no genuine attraction toward a person when I felt them. In those cases, the arousal felt "foreign", as if it were someone else's attraction. It was like it was *happening outside of me*. I knew in these instances that the feeling was originating from what I call *"my desecrated place"*.

I knew something was broken in me when it came to sex, and for this reason, my sexuality was fragile. Although I enjoyed sex, *it was easy to trigger a trauma response by handling me wrongly.* In fact, to maintain my sense of control and get in touch with my genuine desires, I preferred to be *the initiator* in sexual situations. This was important to me, to ensure I was doing what I truly **wanted** to do and that I was not operating out of *my desecrated place*.

Because Keb had been so aggressive toward me, from day one; I'd never had a chance to let my guard down long enough to develop an authentic sense of desire for him. Keb's presence always put me on *high alert*, preventing me from being able to initiate sexual exchanges between us. Keb had taken my power away—not only *my power to choose,* but even **my power to feel**. He doused any genuine attraction that was developing before it could ever mature because of his forcefulness and constant disregard for me not being ready for that type of connection.

Reflections…

I told you earlier that there were two chapters in *The Kiss That Shattered My Soul* that almost killed me to write them. Chapter Twelve is the second of those chapters. Most people think it's ten, *but no,* it's twelve. It is the longest chapter in the book, and I believe that's mainly because once I started drafting it, I didn't know how to stop writing. I felt like I was "bleeding uncontrollably" as I wrote Chapter Twelve, and I didn't know how to stop the flow of blood. That being said, I feel like it is one of the most substantial chapters in the book. I say that because it is so rich in revelation.

In that chapter, I speak about my *desecrated place*—a dark place in my soul, where my trauma wounds build cities constructed of my scabs. *The desecrated place* exists inside of anyone who has experienced trauma, and it's important to understand that. I also show you how I shifted from a bipolar manic episode to a depressive episode. In Chapter Twelve you will learn about "hidden sexual trauma". I'm not talking about *suppressed trauma* that you don't remember. I am talking about trauma that happened before your very eyes that you didn't know how to identify as trauma as it happened, which in my opinion is the worst type of trauma.

So once again, the most painful chapter yields the greatest rewards. Chapter Twelve is a chapter that you could separate from the rest of the book and teach a class on. It is a deep dive into the depraved world of trauma and mental illness; a view that people seldom get to see. As painful as it was for me to write it, I believe it is going to transform many lives. The poem, *Raped of My Dignity,* was as difficult to write as the chapter it correlates to. It is my poetic rendition of how *"hidden sexual trauma"* is birthed. It is a depiction of "consensual sex" that feels more like rape than actual rape. It's so deep; trauma is so deep and so complex…

Raped of My Dignity

This is a desperate surrender
conceived in a desolate space.
In my desecrated place,
I behold your face.

You violate my womb; you awaken my trauma.
You activate my triggers, got me begging for a comma!
A pause… a break… a separation of two clauses,
a distinction between two different causes—
of my volatile reaction to a touch
that should feel good yet instead makes me cringe.
But you don't even notice
while you on your cat-kissing binge!
Eating me like I'm your last meal,
while I'm starving to death
from the way it makes me feel.

The guttural screams of my inner child drive you wild
because they sound like moans to you.
But my heart groans to you,
"PLEASE, STOP!"

This is not what I wanted and far from what I needed.
If you loved me even just a little, you would've conceded.
You promised to love me, but instead you lusted.
I believed in your words, so naively I trusted.

Now you're just another predator,
leaving your bloody handprints on my soul;
another molester who raped me of my dignity,
leaving me empty of what you stole…

Chapter Thirteen

So, That Explains A Lot...

Excerpt from The Kiss That Shattered My Soul

In all my years of painful living, shame, rape, abuse, rejection, and abandonment; *it was the most humiliating thing that had ever happened to me.*

I will never forget how I felt in that moment. It's hard to breathe as I type this out. After all that I'd poured into this man; after all that I had endured; after all that I'd sacrificed to give him what he wanted—*he'd just dismiss me to save his own ass? "This can't be happening. God, please tell me this isn't happening!"* I thought to myself, but I couldn't find the voice to say anything else. I was just too stunned.

Reflections…

There is nothing in the world like the feeling of being used and betrayed by someone you truly believed was a friend. But what's even worse than that is having to come to the conclusion that you never had a friend in the first place. It is one thing to have a falling out with someone you love; it's another thing altogether when you find out the love was only flowing one way—that the feeling was never mutual!

If you are betrayed by someone who loves you, you can hold onto the memories of how they loved you in the past. Even if you don't reconcile, there is value in having been loved. Being loved in any significant capacity adds so much benefit to your life. But when it is the case that the entire relationship was a lie, you have nowhere to reach for comfort. It's like you thought your heart was safely resting on a soft cloud, basking in the sun, surrounded by blue skies. Then suddenly the sun vanishes, the cloud separates underneath you, and you slip through it into a cold black void in space. It's the feeling of just falling, falling, falling, and falling some more—tumbling through cold blackness with no direction and no place to land—the place I call *The Abyss*.

In Chapter Thirteen Keb broke my heart with treachery, betrayal, and humiliation. The betrayal was deep because of the chain of events that led up to it. I was blindsided by it. I'd never been betrayed in that manner; in a way that it caught me so completely off guard. The betrayal was compounded by humiliation because he lied and made me look like a fool in front of people I respected and admired. The pain was paralyzing, and I truly did feel *Like a Used Condom*.

Like a Used Condom is actually a portion and slight adaptation of a track from my self-titled Spoken Word album, "SouLah the Legend". The track is called *Finally, I'm a Woman.* I wrote it in early 2019, as I was still reeling from how broken Keb left me. That was also during the time that I had decided to reclaim my childhood dream of being a creative in the music industry. I was in school for production and engineering at the time. I learned how to produce and record my own tracks and made an entire album. *Finally, I'm a Woman* is a favorite on the album.

Like a Used Condom

My head was in the clouds,
my tummy all full of butterflies.
I never saw your disguise,
because my eyes…
They had star dust in them!

I forgot that everything that glitters ain't gold,
and to most men, I'm just a goal.
I thought you were different, but you weren't.
Your games were just more current.

Smooth like polished bronze,
you were slick-talking like a politician.
While I was hoping and wishing,
you were on a mission,
to add another notch to your belt.
Never mind what I felt,
or what you said you were feeling,
you left my heart reeling.
I should've paid attention to what you were dealing...

The foul stench of your lying breath,
reeking of infidelity and death.
But I plugged my nose,
and I kissed you anyway.
I kissed my soul away.

You took what you came for and then left.
You flushed my affections
down the sewage drain of your mind,
like a used condom.

Chapter Fourteen
And The Loser Is...

Excerpt from The Kiss That Shattered My Soul

I was in such shock that my whole body went limp, and the phone fell out of my hand. I could hear my heart pounding. My throat went dry, and I felt shooting pain in my temples. My breathing was labored and shallow. I WAS HAVING A FULL-BLOWN PANIC ATTACK! I had just awakened when I saw the picture, so I thought I might be dreaming, *having a foul nightmare.* But when I picked the phone up from the floor, it was still there. I was awake; I wasn't dreaming; it was true, and thus...

...It was finished, it was done, ALL HOPE WAS LOST.

And for Keb to be so cruel proved that **this man did not have one blood cell in his entire body that contained any love for me at all!** I had surrendered myself to a man who obviously had not an ounce of respect for me. I could not believe the entire relationship had been a lie. *I felt so stupid, so played, so humiliated, so ashamed, and above all else—SO ANGRY AT MYSELF!*

I DESERVED that outcome.
I had played the fool for this man
and had gotten exactly what I DESERVED!

Reflections...

Chapter Fourteen picks up where Thirteen left off. In fact, they were one chapter in the first manuscript. If *The Kiss That Shattered My Soul* was a movie, Thirteen and Fourteen would be the climax. All things come to a head in these two chapters, and everything becomes clear. Keb took the broken pieces of my heart and smashed them with a sledgehammer; he then took the smashed pieces and burned them in an incinerator; and he took the leftover ashes and scattered them throughout a landfill. This man truly *shattered my existence.*

BUT... I was already cracked before he came, and I offered my heart up for the slaughter. It didn't take much to break me because I was so fragile. It was my responsibility to protect my heart, not his. I gambled away my heart and lost. That was on me.

The poem *Losing Bet* was actually written in 2017, after Keb's betrayal was revealed. When I decided to add poetry to *The Kiss That Shattered My Soul*, I remembered that I had written some poems during my time with Keb. I thought I might want to use a few of them, but they didn't meet my objective of summarizing the correlating chapters. *Losing Bet* was the only one of my writings that made the cut. My jaw literally dropped when I read it. It was perfect because I actually wrote it as a response to the events that I recount in Chapter Fourteen!

On a sidenote... An interesting fact about my 2017 poems is that I recorded them all on a website for poets. Most of them weren't written down anywhere. I created them directly on the web editor. When I went back to look for them for the book, the website had been discontinued and all my poems, dozens of them, were gone! I was so heartbroken.

For some reason, I kept going back to the page repeatedly, as if I could *will it* back up. And *guess what?* It worked! One day I went back to the site and all my poems were there again. I enjoyed reading through my thoughts from that season, but I realized none of them would work for the book except this one. So I recorded it in my book and didn't go back to the site for a few weeks. When I went back to revisit my poems, it was gone again! Like it never existed!!! To this very day, that site no longer exists. *Hmmm...*

Losing Bet

I gambled away my heart.

Then, double or nothing,
I offered up my soul.

You won both,
and then walked away with your winnings.

I have nothing left.

Chapter Fifteen

I'll Never Be Happy Again

Excerpt from The Kiss That Shattered My Soul

I need you to understand that **just because people don't know how to express it, it does not mean they don't care about you.** Everyone is dealing with their own pain, shame, and guilt. *We often take things personally that have nothing to do with us personally.* My ex-husband's hatred toward me was not about me. The girl who beat me up; the "friends" who betrayed me; the babysitter who molested me; the relative who raped me... **None of their actions had anything to do with me!** I was simply "collateral damage" in a war they were fighting within themselves—and such is the case for us all.

I almost killed myself because I didn't understand this. I trusted a broken man to fix my broken life; however, as you can see, you can't keep looking for someone to *rescue you*. To defeat suicidal depression, **I had to learn to be my own hero.** In most of your darkest hours, you will be by yourself. This is not because no one cares, yet instead because those who would want to help you are in their own dark hour!

You must identify at least one thing you deem worth living for. For me, that one thing is believing that God created me for a purpose, and that everything that *happens to me* is really *happening for me*. Whatever that thing ends up being for you, lock in on it as you search for your true happy place. Search for your joy until you find it. **I promise you; it does exist.** But to find it, *you must stop re-assigning your value and handing off the key to your happiness* to people who are not qualified to steward it. NO ONE is qualified to dictate your worth or to decide when you get to smile and enjoy living—***absolutely nobody!***

I am so heartbroken each time I learn of another suicide. It's painful to watch those who are left behind grieve. When people commit suicide, the very people who they were so sure didn't care about them are the ones who hold prayer vigils, create memorials, and start organizations in their honor! The deep depression that those who get left behind must battle can be life-altering. There can even be a chain reaction of other suicides when loved ones who blame themselves can't cope with the guilt and pain.

You need to understand that when a person commits suicide, it's not just their own life they're ending. The pain you are attempting to escape through death becomes someone else's burden to bear, in a way that ends part of their life as well. I often think about how sad my children would be growing up without me. I think about all the people that I've made smile since the day I survived my plans to end my life. I think of all the hugs, kisses, and random acts of kindness I've shared with others that have brightened their lives. I also cherish all the happy memories I've made since then; happiness I thought I would never know. I want you to think about these things too!

I have agonized over how long it has taken to complete this manuscript. According to the latest statistics of 130 suicides per day in the US[1], almost 120,000 people have taken their lives in the time that was required for me to get this book ready! *(And that's only in America!)* I wish I could have saved them all. But if you're reading this today, I hope I can help save you. I know overcoming suicidal depression is difficult. However, I guarantee that if you remember and apply these tips I'm about to share, you will always live to see tomorrow. And one of those tomorrows will eventually lead to ***your best HAPPY LIFE!***

1) *Remember when people hurt you that it's not about you. People hurt you because they're broken! Forgive them, shake it off, and keep going!*

2) *People care about you even when they don't know how to express it! Please know that people are doing their best in their brokenness to love you, just like you're doing your best.*

3) *You will attract the same type of love you give yourself. If you love yourself and are kind to others, you will eventually see that same love show up around you. Patiently cultivate self-love and **I promise you will see it manifest in others!***

4) *Give yourself something positive and worthy to focus on while you discover your own worth, value, and happiness. I strongly encourage you to make developing **a friendship** with GOD part of your positive focus—HE IS CONSTANT!*

5) *And most importantly, never believe the lie that no one will care if you die because **SOMEBODY IS GOING TO MISS YOU WHEN YOU'RE GONE!** Fight to live long enough to prove that to yourself!*

---

[1] https://afsp.org/suicide-statistics/

Reflections...

In Chapter Fifteen of *The Kiss That Shattered My Soul*, I reveal the details of my suicide attempt. If you notice, the *Chapter Fifteen excerpt* is the only one that takes up two pages in this book. That was intentional. If you never get around to reading *The Kiss That Shattered My Soul,* I want to make sure you have these two pages of encouragement to hold on to, to empower and strengthen you.

Sharing my journey with Keb is only a means to an end. Like he used me, I am now using him—I'm using my story with him to help others who are suffering from depression, suicidal thoughts, and toxic relationships. I want to help people see the correlation between the three, and I want to help them break the cycle. My relationship with Keb just so happens to be the perfect point of reference to help me illustrate my points.

I understand that reading about people's depression and trauma can be triggering for others who are suffering from similar issues. I don't want to just tell my *sad story* and leave you triggered. I also want to show you how to navigate your way out of your own sad story to a happier ending. I am very passionate about helping people overcome suicidal thoughts to live another day. After seven suicide attempts—I DO NOT DESERVE TO BE HERE. I didn't appreciate my life, and yet God still spared it. I'm going to make that count for the rest of my days!

I owe it to my kids, to myself, to the universe, and to humanity to MAKE MY LIFE MATTER. To anyone who may be feeling like, *"I'll Never Be Happy Again,"* I want you to know that *My Soul Lives On*, and yours can too!

My Soul Lives On

Though life won't be perfect,
and I'll sometimes be sad,
after midnight comes dawn,
and good comes after bad.

So, I will write my poems,
and I will sing my songs.
And when I miss the mark,
I will right my wrongs.

I will love people freely,
and I won't be afraid.
But I'll love myself more,
to become what I've prayed.

I choose to be happy,
I will laugh and I will play.
And I will make new plans,
for a brand-new day.

No more tears,
I've finally stopped crying.
There comes an endpoint,
in the process of dying.

And when death is complete,
resurrection can begin.
It's then my soul realizes,
it has survived once again!

Chapter Sixteen

Suicidal Relationships

Excerpt from The Kiss That Shattered My Soul

When you install a software update on a computer, it is often necessary to remove the previous version first. All the folders, commands, and functions of the previous version must be permanently deleted for the new version to run effectively. From my story, I hope you can see that ***it is often a previous version of us that is secretly running the program!***

The problem with the human soul is that we don't know how to completely "uninstall previous versions of ourselves". We tend to have multiple outdated versions running all at once. The new version, with all the latest updates, bells, and whistles, will be running without a hitch. Then we bump into a person, or get into a situation that triggers an old, damaged version. Without warning or understanding, our mode of operation switches to that outdated, corrupt version. We will continue to dysfunction in this old mode until we realize we're "not running right". Unfortunately, by then, the entire program may have crashed; and this can impact our entire operating system!

Reflections...

As I think on it now, maybe I should have titled Chapter Sixteen *The Conclusion*. I didn't think of it as a conclusion because I know this story will continue in *Part 2* of the *Taking Your Power Back!* series. But from a literary standpoint, without any consideration for a *Part 2* book that doesn't exist at the moment, Chapter Sixteen is definitely the conclusion of *The Kiss That Shattered My Soul*—and a good one at that.

There is no story to tell in Chapter Sixteen. The entire chapter is a sober reflection of how badly I screwed up, why I screwed up, and what I learned from it all. One of my favorite teaching points is in Chapter Sixteen. I use the analogy of computer software to explain how former versions of ourselves linger in *the hidden self*, waiting for an opportunity to take over and be relevant.

I introduce *the hidden self* in Chapter Six, by the way. If you haven't read *The Kiss That Shattered My Soul* yet, please be prepared to take copious notes and get a keen understanding of *the hidden self*. That revelation is mind-transforming. If you have read it and didn't catch its significance—GO BACK AND READ IT AGAIN UNTIL YOU FULLY ABSORB IT! *The hidden self* will be a running theme throughout this series and a very important part of learning how to **Take Your Power Back!**

At any rate, in Chapter Sixteen I teach you to discover and root out the elements of the hidden self. Or in other words, *"how to uninstall old soulware"*. I prepare you to take the next step in your healing with realistic expectations about the process. I think a lot of "self-help gurus" do people a grave injustice by giving off the impression that reinventing yourself can be done with a few affirmations, some daily meditation, and "choosing to be happy".

I'm sorry! But give me a freaking break! It took decades to get into the mess that you have become. It's going to take some time to work your way to the version of yourself that you want to be. You are going to screw up plenty more times. You're going to want to quit again. And you will question yourself, fail, and probably revisit your old ways a time or two... *or 10, or 20, or 50...* Hopefully it won't be that many times, but please know that it's all a normal part of the process. It's okay. The important thing is that YOU JUST KEEP GOING!

Outdated Soulware

Things were going along perfectly splendid.
My new upgrades were working just as intended.
I had new features and added benefits,
had even worked out some old glitches and detriments.
I was faster, more efficient, more functional,
and had a sleek new design.
Baby, you couldn't tell me nothing,
because I had updated and elevated my mind!

But there was a problem.
I installed my upgrade on top of a previous version,
that lurked in the trash bin of my soul and wanted incursion.
I tried to remove it but could only replace it.
I could reposition it but never erase it!
That old version was mad that I tried to do away with it.
And I had the nerve to not take it seriously and tried to play with it!

Without warning it was reactivated,
when I ran into a familiar command
from an old demand.
A demand for a man to rescue my heart and be my validation.
And suddenly, that old version took over my operations!

But I never knew it...
I kept performing as if I was still running with my new upgrades.
Didn't notice the switch until my whole life was in a complete downgrade.
And now I'm down—down and out.
Out here looking stupid, played, and tired.
That old soulware showed me who's boss
when I thought it had expired!

So, here's my tip to you.
Uninstall all previous versions of yourself,
before you try to act brand new!

THE INTERMISSION
Make Your Pain Pay!

Excerpt from The Kiss That Shattered My Soul

Here is the most essential factor in getting back up: **Learn how to MAKE YOUR PAIN PAY!** This philosophy has been a **master key** to my ability to thrive through pain because the fact is, THERE IS NO WAY you can permanently stop pain in your life. The only way to *guarantee* that you never lose again, or experience pain again, is to die. *BUT...* I have an even better solution than death—*make your pain pay, turn your losses into lessons, and your lessons into legacy!*

You are going to lose sometimes; you are going to hurt sometimes; but the recovery process is sure to strengthen you! That is why today, after a lifetime of struggling with suicidal depression, I have finally defeated that demon of death with a single weapon. It is what I call *My Pain Response*. Before I used to let pain defeat me. I allowed it to bully me, kick my butt, and trigger my "trauma response"! Yet henceforth, now, and forevermore, my principal response to pain is to ask myself the question, *"HOW CAN I WIN FROM THIS?"*

After I have finished grieving *(grieving is important),* I determine how to capitalize off my pain by asking myself these questions:

- *What can I learn from this?*
- *How can I use this experience to get closer to who I want to be?*
- *How can I turn this around in my favor?*
- *How can I use this as an investment in my future significance?*
- ***HOW CAN I MAKE MY PAIN PAY?***
- ***HOW CAN I WIN FROM THIS?!***

Please believe me when I tell you, THE PAIN RESPONSE WORKS!

Reflections...

One day, in August of 2017, I was sitting in my car bawling. I can't recall what I was crying about. *Who knows?* It could have been anything because that was my posture almost 24/7. I was always crying, in between my manic bursts of energy and inspiration. I was either manic or crying. Those were my only two modes of operation at that time, and that day I was in crying mode.

My crying wasn't normal. The sadness would take over me when I cried. My entire body would grieve with me. I would feel literal physical pain. My heart would feel as if it were going to explode inside my chest. My head would throb. My bones and joints would ache. It was a desperate kind of feeling, and it seemed like an inescapable sadness—*like I would just cry forever, and ever, and ever...*

(OMG, I just burst into tears writing that. It's heartbreaking to remember how awful that feels!)

At any rate, on that particular day Yahweh, my God, spoke to me very clearly. I heard Him say to me, *"Make Your Pain Pay."*

I stopped crying and said, *"Huh? What do you mean Daddy?"* I'd never heard that before and I hadn't a clue what He meant.

He responded to me. *"Don't you understand? Your tears are like currency. I collect every single one of them and store them in your account. My Daughter, you are a very wealthy woman. With all the tears you've cried, you're wealthier than a billionaire. So tell your pain to write you a check! Make Your Pain Pay!"*

Just in case anyone may be wondering—Yahweh does not speak to me in an audible voice. And He seldom uses verbatim language in a way that can be translated word-for-word. He usually speaks in a heart language. It is a communication between His heart and mine, and because of our closeness I understand what He's conveying to me. It's hard to translate sometimes, though.

But this conversation was one of those rare times when God used express English words to make a statement to me. He used words that He wanted me to remember exactly as He'd spoken them, and that He wanted me to stand on. He said expressly, clearly, and in verbatim words, ***"Make Your Pain Pay!"*** And I realize now that those weren't *just words.* It was a mandate for how to live my life. It was instruction on how to reclaim my happiness and *Take My Power Back,* and I strive to live those words every day!

Make Your Pain Pay!

Your pain is an investment, your tears are like currency,
so put them in the bank because life won't be worry-free!
The more trials you face, the richer you become,
because true wealth isn't in money, but in what you overcome.

When it's time to be great,
you'll need to write yourself a check,
from the account of your past traumas,
and you'll be like, *"What the heck!"*—
when you see that colossal balance,
and realize what you have in you,
where you've been, what you've accomplished,
and the awe of what you've been through!

So, when life gives you hurt,
don't look for the simplest,
escape from the pain.
Just say, *"How can I win from this?"*

Teach yourself to capitalize and maximize the tears you cry.
Just begin to fantasize and visualize that winning high!
Cuz, Baby! You're filthy rich,
from all the dirty hands,
that tried to leave you in a ditch.
They buried you,
not understanding that you're a seed.
Now that you've sprouted and taken root,
you're getting watered every time you bleed!

So, the truth of the matter is,
you're wealthy in the most secure way.
You've got **hidden treasure inside**, so...
...Make Your Pain Pay!

Did you find this book helpful, enjoyable, or insightful?

Please stop and take a moment to leave a 5-star review on Amazon! It means so much!

Please visit https://www.amazon.com/review/create-review/edit?ie=UTF8&channel=glance-detail&asin=1734663316

Or scan the QR below

Laneen "SouLah the Legend" Haniah

Laneen A. Haniah is a Creative Influencer and entertainer better known as *SouLah the Legend.* She has more than 40 years' experience as an award-winning author and keynote speaker. She has spoken at over 300 events and has six published titles. In addition, she is a songwriter, producer, poet, comedian, model, actor, journalist, editor, and podcaster. She is founder of **Don't Miss Out!,** which is a non-profit dedicated to emotional health, trauma recovery, and suicide prevention. She has also started a movement called **Healing Black Love**. *Healing Black Love* is an outreach to restore Black relationships, the Black family, and the Black Community. The movement was founded on the principles detailed in her best-selling book, **How to Love a Black Man: RESPECT HIM.**

Suffering unrelenting emotional and physical pain throughout her life led to multiple suicide attempts. However, SouLah the Legend is now happy, whole, and moving forward like the world is hers! Crossing over age 50 and having successfully raised seven children, she refuses to let anything stop her. She embraces every day to redeem the years lost to sickness, depression, people-pleasing, and unhealed trauma; and she passionately pursues her purpose. SouLah's path has cultivated a hunger to encourage others to live a meaningful and liberated life, and she leads by example.

She reminds people every day, through her *Journey to Self-Mastery* series—***Only You Can Make Your Life Matter!***

Laneen Haniah is set apart by the relevance of her firsthand experience and her unique and diverse delivery of content, through her compelling books, captivating speeches, and distinctive music productions. As owner of ***Inspired Legacy Publishing*** *and* ***Lah Lah Land Studios,*** SouLah the Legend is transforming lives. She elevates and expands others daily, through her comedy and empowering social media content. There is no question that she is determined to live legendary and leave legacy. ***SouLah the Legend is a RELEVANT VOICE, speaking the universal language of the soul!***

For booking, purchases, or more information, visit www.soulah.me or text 404-565-4569.

SouLah the Legend—

A RELEVANT VOICE,
speaking the universal language of the soul...

SUICIDE AND CRISIS LIFELINE

Dial or text 988 or visit www.988lifeline.org

If you are experiencing mental health-related distress or are worried about a loved one who may need crisis support, connecting with a trained crisis counselor is confidential, free, and available 24/7/365!

ALWAYS DIAL 911 IN AN IMMEDIATE EMERGENCY!

Other Resources:

Crisis Text Line
Text "HELLO" to 741741
Available 24 hours a day, seven days a week throughout the U.S. serving anyone, in any type of crisis.

Veterans Crisis Line
Call 1-800-273-TALK (8255) and press 1 or text to 838255
Use Veterans Crisis Chat on the web https://www.veteranscrisisline.net/get-help-now/chat/
The Veterans Crisis Line is a free and confidential service available to all veterans, even if they are not registered with the VA or enrolled in VA healthcare!

Contact social media outlets directly if you are concerned about a friend's social media updates or **dial 911** in an emergency.

For Laneen Haniah's personally created and/or recommended resources for mental health and suicide prevention awareness, please visit www.irefusetomissout.com or scan the QR code below.

Resources for Mental Health and Depression

According to The National Institute of Mental Health 52.9 million Americans are suffering from some type of mental health issue. That is 1 out of every 5 adults! I felt so alone as I went through my healing process, but you don't have to—please don't do it alone!

NIMH *(The National Institute of Mental Health)*
www.nimh.nih.gov
Crisis Text Line Text "HELLO" to 741741
Available 24 hours a day, seven days a week throughout the U.S. serving anyone, in any type of crisis.

NAMI *(National Alliance on Mental Illness)*
www.nami.org/help
Call 1-800-950-NAMI (6264), text "HelpLine" to 62640,
email helpline@nami.org, or chat at www.nami.org/help
Monday through Friday, 10 a.m.–10 p.m. EST. NAMI HelpLine volunteers will answer questions, offer support, and provide practical next steps for anyone suffering from anxiety, PTSD, mood disorders, eating disorders, schizophrenia, and other mental health challenges.

The Depression Project
https://thedepressionproject.com/
A social support community for those suffering from depression. The depression project can offer support and helpful resources that will *"guide you from the storm to the sun."*

Resources for Victims of Sexual Trauma

Have you been a victim of sexual abuse or rape? YOU ARE NOT ALONE! According to RAINN, sexual violence happens every 68 seconds in the US! Please take advantage of these free resources to aid your healing process.

RAINN *(Rape, Abuse & Incest National Network)*
Call 1-800-656-HOPE (4673) or visit www.RAINN.org for chat.
RAINN is the nation's largest anti-sexual violence organization and operates the National Sexual Assault Hotline, available 24/7. You can also download the RAINN mobile app.

The Victim Connect Resource Center
Call or Text 1-855-484-2846 or visit www.victimconnect.org for chat service.
Available Weekdays 8 a.m. to 5 p.m. (EST)
VictimConnect is a referral helpline where crime victims can learn about their rights and options confidentially and compassionately.

DoD Safe HelpLine
Call 1-877-995-5247 or visit chat at https://safehelpline.org
100% confidential sexual assault support for members of the military community. Call, chat, or download the mobile app 24/7. Also get help for reporting retaliation!

Other books by Laneen A. Haniah

SUICIDAL LOVE: *The Kiss That Shattered My Soul*

Help, My Child Doesn't Want to Live!
How to reach your depressed, suicidal teen

Suicidal Love:
A Book of Reflective Thoughts and Poetry

How to Love a Black Man:
RESPECT HIM-2025 Edition

This Is Me!
I Don't Need Your Permission
(New memoir celebrating 50 years of life!
Pre-order now.)

Find eBooks, bundles, and specials on the author's website

www.soulah.me

www.ingramcontent.com/pod-product-compliance
Lightning Source LLC
Chambersburg PA
CBHW081552040426
42448CB00016B/3295